Adventures (

Pennsylv

MW00423434

Copyright 2014

Matthew & Marlene Snader

PO Box 988

Anchor Point, AK 99556

Photography by Matthew and Marlene Snader

Maps by Google Maps

Forward by Josh Snader

Published by Online Advertising, LLC

Printed in the United States of America

ISBN 978-1-4951-3489-0

Future "Adventures of a Traveling Dog Salesman" that you may enjoy:

- Return to Alaska: Building a Cabin on the Final Frontier (release scheduled for spring of 2015)

- Flying Alaska: 10 Easy Steps to Flying a Float Plane (landing is the tricky part)

- Fishing Alaska: Halibut and Salmon Fishing on a Budget

- Alaska Moose Hunting on a Budget

- Alaska Brown Bear Hunting on a Budget

- How to Make a Million Dollars in Alaska (the production of this books seems in doubt at the moment)

- Living "off the grid" in Alaska

Note: Future titles may be added, changed or canceled, due to life experiences of the author, given they are meant to be non fiction titles.

Contents

Meet the Snader family:

Contrary to what some folks think, I actually have a job. Yes, I'm actually a bit of a traveling dog salesman. No, I don't go door to door with a brief case full of dogs. My job is to run the advertising programs for several pet classified websites, where people with puppies can place listings. We mostly advertise dogs, but we just sold a "litter" of pet piglets, so you never know what will happen. The limo is used to advertise one our sites, I'll let you guess which one.

Marlene and I homeschool our children, which we find rewarding. Children learn better in a one on one environment. We also are Bible believing Christians, and want to live our lives in a way that points to Jesus Christ, our redeemer and Lord.

Our family enjoys traveling, finding it educational and fun. Our goal is to eventually visit all 50 states. We are about 4 states away from reaching that goal. We also enjoy the outdoors, love hiking, hunting, and fishing. (some of us more than others)

We currently have 6 children, although in this trip only 5 are mentioned. That is because Mary Kate was born in August of 2014, and our trip took place June-July of 2013.

If you have any questions or comments, please email them to matt@AmericanGunDogs.com.

Thank you,

The Snader Family

" But let all those that put their trust in thee rejoice: let them ever shout for joy, because thou defendest them: let them also that love thy name be joyful in thee." Psalms 5:11

Matt & Marlene Snader

Lana, Desiree, Shane, Kallia (holding Mary Kate) and Samantha

Forward by Josh Snader

Sometimes exploring can make one itch. Sometimes literally, if you are exploring a fiberglass insulation plant or crawling through a field of poison ivy, but sometimes it's a bit deeper than that. The itch usually begins developing when you are looking at pictures of Glacier National Park or the Grand Teton mountains. It's so majestic, you just want to hop into the picture and start climbing over the horizon. But you can't. It's just a picture on a calendar stuck to the wall of your cubicle. Suddenly, a part of your soul that is flattened down by all the reasonable responsibilities and excuses in your life, starts to kick and squirm, making you all itchy and uncomfortable.

The itching continues until one day you have enough of it and organize a trip to somewhere awesome with some friends. You are so happy and excited since you now have a goal and an objective in life, other than trying to be the fastest hamster on the wheel. You are happy because you are going to experience breathtaking beauty in reality. You are excited because you will soon be experiencing the tangible reality that somehow sets the intangible parts of you all aglow.

You go there, enjoy yourself, and come home. You scratched the itch and it feels better. Aaaah.

Soon enough, however, you start to feel the itch again. The itch to explore is a condition that is never cured, and only gets worse the more it's treated.

A lot of people don't understand the condition of exploration. Your employer, (or in Matt's case, employees) especially, will be asking things like:

"You're traveling again? Didn't you just get home from (put a place in here) just a few months ago?"

Your parents and married friends will be like:

"Isn't it time to settle down and get on with life?"

Regardless, a prevailing mindset that comes with your return from the land down yonder is this:

"I'm glad you got that traveling bug out of your system. Now, here's some stuff to catch up on."

That's a sign that they just don't get it. A traveling bug can't be squashed. Unknown to them, you are already planning another trip in the back of their mind, you just don't know where to yet. The thought of sticking it out in a cubicle for another twenty years crushes your free spirited soul like an obese elephant sitting his haunches down on an aluminum can. That's the exact kind of crunching sound a crushed sense of adventure sounds like.

However, like an aluminum can, your sense of adventure can be crushed, flattened, and buried, but it's non-corrosive and pretty much lasts forever in some form, despite being in the bottom of a landfill.

And soon, it repeats itself. You find yourself boarding an airplane bound for some part of somewhere you've never been before. Or, you find yourself driving all night, bleary eyed and twitching from the copious amounts of cheap coffee you're chugging, just so you can go hiking for a day. Then you turn around and head back towards civilization again, all for the sake of some job and lifestyle you don't even really want.

You begin to get depressed. No matter how many places you've found, there's always more to discover. No matter how many people you've met, there's billions more living their lives, never to cross paths with yours. No matter how many times you've seen the same sun set in different places, you still want to get a thrill out of seeing it rise again somewhere else.

Traveling is merely dumping fuel on the fire of exploration. No matter how much money you have and no matter how much time you are allotted, you will never, ever visit every place on earth.

And I'm beginning to realize that's a good thing. For the love of exploration is a love that will never die. Discovery isn't a goal to be completed, but a continuing series of events that compounds on itself as you go through life. There will always be something, someone, or somewhere that is utterly astounding and that will excite that part of your soul that leaps at the chance of discovery.

The itch of exploration is something personal. People can and have explored a majority of the world. But you haven't. And, unlike many people, you aren't content with pictures in a magazine or a blog. In fact, other adventurer's experiences do nothing to satisfy the thirst of discovery in your own soul. They only give you a desire to go see it for yourself. Personally experiencing something awesome on your own is the definition of discovery. Scuba diving looks like fun, but you haven't discovered it until you've done it on your own. I have my SSI certification now. People have gone scuba diving long before I found it, but I've only discovered it recently. I've discovered SCUBA because I've personally experienced it. No one else can discover things for you. No words will sufficiently describe an experience to the point that you won't discover it *more* doing it for yourself.

Discovery is an infinite, never ending process, yet it's a personally fulfilling experience. What are you discovering today?

Josh Snader

Route Map for our 2013 Alaska Trip

One inaccuracy in the map below is Google Maps refused to include the "Top of the World" highway in the trip layout. This runs between "G" (North Pole, AK) and "H" (Dawson City) on the map below. The reason is this is closed during winter months, and it was in fact winter when I generated this trip map.

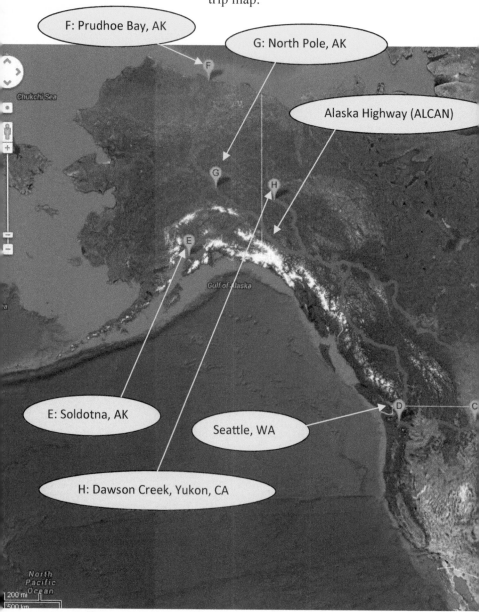

F: Prudhoe Bay, AK

G: North Pole, AK

Alaska Highway (ALCAN)

E: Soldotna, AK

Seattle, WA

H: Dawson Creek, Yukon, CA

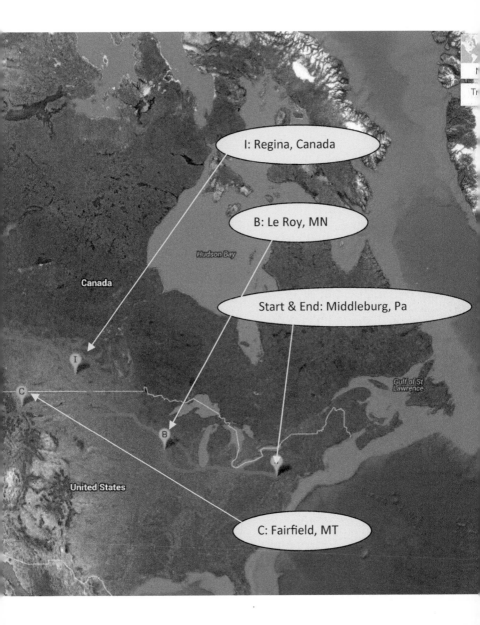

I: Regina, Canada

B: Le Roy, MN

Start & End: Middleburg, Pa

C: Fairfield, MT

Chapter 1

"The Limo" vs Mini Van

Painting a limousine camouflage. Driving it multiple times from Pennsylvania to Alaska. You may have some questions like, why? And how did you ever get your wife to agree to such a thing? Have you lost your mind? And so on. Keep reading, and you will find out why, and the history behind such innovation.

First, lets walk you through clearing your mind of preconceived ideas and other rubbish. Avoid being like the bullheaded Roman Inquisition, mindlessly attacking Galileo over the thought of the sun being the center of our Solar System. Look at some cold hard facts, like what characteristics an ideal family vehicle should have:

- Good fuel mileage
- Have lots of room
- Good towing capacity
- Cheap
- Easy to repair
- Flexible seating

You would think most common sense, intelligent, practical people would agree an ideal family vehicle would have all the above characteristics. Lets compare a limousine to a mini van, going over that list. Having owned several mini vans, and several limousines, I feel I can make educated comparisons. You may be shocked at the results.

Note: Since we are talking about used vehicles, results may vary.

Limousine verses Mini Van

1. **Fuel Mileage:** I have owned four mini vans, all Dodge Caravans. (I once raced one in an off road "tuff trucks" event-I don't count that one) Fuel mileage ranged between 16-19 mpg. My Lincoln Town Car Limousines? As low as 16 mpg- but I achieved 20+ mpg many times, getting 22.8 mpg on several tanks. Looks like a Limo takes this one.

2. **Lots of Room:** A Grand Caravan has some wiggle room behind the back seat for luggage, but stuff 8 people in, and mini vans seem awful "mini". Our stretch limo, however, hauled 14 people from New York to Ontario. Limo takes 2.

3. **Towing Capacity:** There is no comparison in this category. Stretched Lincoln's have a V8 engine, truck transmission and rear axle, and adjustable air shocks. Mini vans? Tiny 4 and 6 cylinder engines, with puny front transaxles that are sure to break. Limousines reign supreme here.

4. **Cheap:** Mini Vans seem to have the upper hand here. My first mini van (beside the tuff truck one) I traded a computer for, the others varied in price from $500 to $1,000. My first limo I paid $1,500 for, the second one, a salty $2,800. The Mini Van wins this round.

5. **Easy to Repair:** At first glance under the hood, it would seem the mini van wins this one. However, once the wrenches come out, the van falls by the wayside. While there is more room under the hood of a mini van, incompetent engineering quickly minimizes the extra room. The intelligent rear wheel drive layout of the limo allows for easy to access to the transmission and drive axle.

6. **Flexible Seating:** Most mini vans allow for the seats to be easily removed for extra cargo room. However, limousines play the trump card-more seating room, and more cargo room

without the need to take the seats out. Most limousines have what is called a "J seat". This seat runs along the side and front of the car, giving plenty of leg room, as well as plenty of luggage room in the trunk. There is no question-the Limo takes this category.

Limos: 5, Mini Vans: 1.

Conclusion: The value of limousines makes open minded min van owners blush and hang their head in shame at their lack of frugalness. The 4.6 V8 in Lincolns is also shared by the Ford Mustang. This means you can get a wide array of performance parts and accessories. The fact the Crown Victoria is also built on the same platform also allows you to find useful accessories like brush guards, etc. Mini Vans however, share no useful platform with anything.

Frivolous rat wagon

Verses

Practical, useful, luxury workhorse

Actually, my first brush involving cheap vehicles and modifications goes back to when I was 12 or 13. My cousin, Paul, got a free 1970's era pickup of some sort. We took the doors off, and drove it through his parents farm fields at a high rate of speed. Well, it was only 20 mph or so, but even that feels fast when your driving over ditches and hitting trees. Looking back, taking the doors off was a terrible idea, but hindsight is 20/20.

I bought my first car for $150 when I was 14. It was a 1981 Mustang, a wretched, piece of junk mustang, one that continued to be so no matter how much time and money I put into it. It featured a 200 cubic inch inline 6. I later bought a 1978 Ford Granada with a larger, 260 cubic inch inline 6. For some unknown reason, I decided to put the Granada engine in the Mustang. We actually got this contraption to work, however it proved to be hideously unreliable. The transmission gears would randomly jam, and the only way to free them would be to crawl underneath and beat on the shift linkage with a hammer. An exhaust leak also left the occupants of the Mustang smelling like a small garage.

Astonishingly, I started dating a beautiful young lady named Marlene around 2001. Even more astonishing is that she later agreed to marry me. Soon after we started dating, I bought an old van from her dad for $75. She later recalls that she should have heeded that as an omen of things to come. (she assumed that after I "grew up" I would pickup the bad habit of driving later model "normal" vehicles)

Assuming it was my rugged good looks, I recently asked Marlene why she was attracted to me. She told me it was my "sense of adventure". Oh, ah, ok. I suppose there could be worse things, like "how fast I could smoke cigarettes". *

I do admit to having a relatively normal car during our dating years, besides the old $75 van. The "normal" car was a

*I don't smoke cigarettes and never have, this is just an illustration.

a canary yellow 1994 Mustang GT. Unlike my other miserable excuses for Mustangs, this car actually ran like a real Mustang, having a 5.0L V8 engine and 5 speed transmission. I found myself bored with this car, however, as it was "too nice" for spray painting or welding things on it, and driving in fields was out of the question. Sure, driving fast is fun, but it wasn't really my forte. (although I did enjoy "smoking the tires".) But Marlene did like the car, so we kept it until a few years after we were married, and when faced with a personal financial Armageddon, we sold it.

I was friends with a car dealer, and I used to borrow limousines from him on a regular basis. We would take these limo's to concerts or valentine's banquets, etc. Small things like taking them through fast food drive throughs we found amusing. Coincidently, these were all stretched Lincoln Town Cars. (you can get stretched Cadillac's, Hummers, or whatever anymore) Every limo I purchased has been a Lincoln Town Car, simply because that is what I happened to find cheap.

I had quite a few vintage Ford vans, which of course got custom paint jobs:

I purchased my first Limousine, a 1990 Lincoln Town Car, off of Ebay in late 2007 for $1,500. We used the limo for a variety of things, from starting a dog transportation business, to using it to promote the dog classified website LancasterPuppies.com.

Unfortunately that limo was later viciously vandalized by alleged extreme animal rights folks, aka terrorists. (I had the audacity to promote selling puppies with the limo) Or maybe it was just some wayward teenagers. The PA state police investigated, but the perpetrators were never found. However, that is another story. (It did make the WGAL Channel 8 evening news)

I think it is accurate to consider animal rights activists as terrorists, because we have gotten quite a bit of hate mail from these zealous individuals. Threats of violence and destruction of property, demands we rot in the underworld, etc. Another example, activists were applauding the violent destruction of our limo on the WGAL news website in the story comments. Of course, I'm not advocating animal abuse, but these folks would consider eating a hamburger an atrocity. It's hard to reason with such people. Impossible, actually.

The smashed limo left a void, that only a limo can fill. So early 2013, I was still advertising puppies, and I happened to stumble across another limo for sale in Quarryville, Pa. It actually was advertised as a potential trade for a backhoe or bull dozer. Not having either, I called the fellow selling it, and asked if they would take cash. He decided he would, and the rest was history.

The second Limo, a 1992 Lincoln Town Car:

The untimely demise of my first limo, a 1990 Lincoln:

I was jubilant with the purchase of another limo. Looking back, I asked Marlene how I ever convinced her we should buy another limo. Here reply was "You never did convince me". Uh oh. Well, I do remember a few tense moments when I brought the car home. If I recall, painting it camouflage didn't help the situation, nor did the purchase of a $300 brush guard for the front.

Buying the limo also solved a short term problem for Marlene's uncle, Ivan Martin. He was scheduled to give a lecture on Creation in Ontario, Canada, and being an old order Mennonite, had no car. He also wanted to bring several family members along. We volunteered to drive the Limo, and after some consideration, he agreed that was the practical thing to do. If you have never driven a limousine filled with old order Mennonites across the Canadian border, you should. From the reaction of the border guards, I got the impression this was unusual.

The limo performed well on the trip to Ontario and back. The only small glitch was the heater and defrost stopped working. Oh, and the thermostat also gave out, which was replaced with a $20 one from Canadian tire. I have learned to really like Canadian Tire stores-especially the trip where I had 5 or 6 trailer tires blow out in one week's time. But that is for another book. The Limo would also randomly beep several times, each hour. After this happened several times, and nothing went wrong, I was forced to assume that this was a good news indicator, and not a bad one.

The US—Canada border

The lack of a heater turned out to be a somewhat severe disadvantage, considering the temperatures were

AmericanGunDogs.com blog post by Matt on 3/16/2013:

Fiscal restraint, buying limousines, and other compatible habits

I woke up this morning with a new limousine in my driveway. Well, it's not quite new, in a year or two I can put classic tags on it. Now some uneducated folks might ask "what on earth are you doing with a limousine?!", since I'm not a politician or an agent for the Amish mafia. By uneducated folks, I mean those who may not have read my earlier blog entry about how limos make great hunting vehicles.

How much did I pay for this fine piece of automotive history, you might ask? Well, that's the beauty of it. I leased this puppy for $95 a month, $0 down. At the end of the lease I can just keep the car. That's the price of a tank of gas (in my Ford Expedition), the cost of a bill board for a few days, or several bags of potatoes. This 30 foot marvel has a V-8 engine, seats 11, can get 20 mpg, and has a trunk big enough to fit a horse in it. It can easily pull a boat and trailer. It is the definition of thriftiness and practicality all wrapped up in one package. (Folks with mini vans are probably blushing in shame at their lack of thrift as they read this)

Naturally, some of you are probably wondering how I leased a limo, since it's more likely to get a loan officer to gallop around his office kicking his feet in the air like a wild gazelle than to actually approve something, especially for a situation a little out of the ordinary. For example:

The other day I walked into the local bank, trying to get a home equity loan on my old house, which I am trying to sell. (I was trying to pay down the mortgage which had a higher interest rate than the HELOC) You would have thought I was randomly proposing to a nun. The loan officer suspiciously glanced at me. "Hmm so you want a heloc?" he asked. I explained why, and he said "your not making any money on this house like renting it, right?". I explained, no this house was a total drag and I was certainly not making any money on it. "Good" he said, "we can't give out loans if your using the property to make money". Ok...that would explain all the foreclosures you hear about, but anyway.

Next he said, "we'll have to write this up as a vacation home". Ok, sure, but I live 2 miles away from it. Then I mentioned I want to sell the house. He reacted in astonishment, "Why would you want to sell your vacation house that is a total drag and you live 2 miles away from?". Ah, beats me. So he had to call some guy in another office and told me "we can't give loans for houses that you want to sell". **Continued on next page ->**

a bit on the brisk side. Consoling them about the fact we were not in a horse and buggy seemed ineffective. However, everyone survived and seemed none the worse for wear.

The Limo at our host's house in Ontario, Canada:

One caution about driving limos to visit conservative Canadians, is they don't like limousines in their driveway. Our host had us park the Limo at a neighbors house, while he hosted the speaking engagement. They assured us they didn't think Limos were bad, but they were concerned others might. I did point out the car was over 20 years old, but they still thought it would be better parked out of sight. That's ok, no offense taken.

AmericanGunDogs.com blog post by Matt on 3/16/2013:

Fiscal restraint, buying limousines, and other compatible habits cont

Ok, well that last thing he said made some sense but nothing else did. Anyway, I digress. (If you want to live near Troxelville, PA, shoot me an email.) Editors Note: That house is now sold

So how did I work out a lease agreement? Simple, I just called a friend and said "are you tired of getting 0.01% interest at the bank with their miserable CDs? Lease this car to me and get a better return". Now, under normal circumstances I loathe not paying cash for cars. A quick look in my driveway will verify this principle. However I am not against leasing business equipment, and it will be very obvious in a few days that this car is to promote "AmericanGunDogs.com". Just wait and see...

What are my plans for this car? Simple, I'm going to paint it camouflage, and letter "AmericanGunDogs.com" along each side of it. I'll drive it around and get more than my $95 for that month back in advertising in short order. For example, the cheapest bill board I could find along Route 11-15 (a main route here in central Pa) costs $600 a month, and you have to commit to several months at a shot. Three months and you blow $1,800. Studies also show that a new bill board loses it's effect in one to two weeks of being put up. Regular traffic gets used to seeing them and stops looking. And you certainly can't take a bill board on a road trip.

Before:

After:

Chapter 2

Painting "The Limo" Camouflage

Some folks mistakenly think it is hard to paint a car camouflage. It's actually very easy, if you get a runner, you just sand it down and hit it with another color. There is also the misconception that you need "real car paint". Regular spray paint cans from the hardware store will do just fine, although real car paint does last much longer.

Before painting the limo, we needed to strip all the chrome off of it. I expected this to be easy, but it was anything but. There were also a bunch of annoying rubber strips stuck to the car, which smoke like mad if you throw them in an outdoor furnace. We also discovered that shiny silver strip running along the bottom was glued on, as in covered with glue. We needed to peel that off, inch by inch. As a practical person, I personally feel chrome is a complete waste of money and should be replaced by something worthwhile like camouflage.

My good friend Arlan, at "Clark Hill Service Center" in Mt. Pleasant Mills, Pa, kindly let me paint the limo in his garage. He also helped me mount the brush guard, which was extremely helpful, as the bumper cover took a bit of work to get off.

Below you can see our first attempt at shooting camouflage. In this picture, it is not finished, it needs more spots and twigs. We also replaced the ugly stock Lincoln rims with some rims and tires off of a 1995 Ford Explorer. (picture below still has stock rims on) I was shocked they fit, but Lincoln Town Cars have huge wheel wells.

After some more experimenting, we got a pattern going that we thought was acceptable, and I lettered the car with 11 inch high letters that read "AmericanGunDogs.com".

My brother in law, Paul, owned a grocery store called "Beavertown Guns & Grocery" along route 522, between Middleburg and Beavertown. He graciously let me park the limo along the busy route, to promote our website "AmericanGunDogs.com". This attracted the attention of the local newspaper, which ran a front page article on the Limo. Naturally I thought this was a newsworthy event, but my brother insisted it was a sign that not much happened in Snyder County...

Chapter 3—Leaving for Alaska

Some people, especially those that like to plan everything in advance, the types that figure how many sheets of toilet paper they use a week, would be shocked to hear that our first Alaska trip was not planned real far in advance. The truth is, it was planned years in advance, but not in the same way "bean counters" plan. After all, we had casually discussed driving to Alaska before, and that is sort of planning.

The real Alaska discussions started in late May of 2013, after we finally managed to sell our old house. I'm not sure if Marlene or myself mentioned it first, but before we knew what happened, Marlene was looking up "driving the Alcan highway" on Google. At that time we discovered the best time to make the trip was in June, which was a few days away. Worried that something like a car repair bill or other unpleasant, unexpected expense would come up, we decided to leave as soon as possible. After all, we had a fuel efficient car we all fit in, a job I could do while on the road, some money for gas, and good health. What more could we ask for? And how often do you hear people on their deathbed wish they would have "saved up more money"?

Our friends and family put on some good acting skills, attempting to feign incredulous as we casually mentioned our decision to leave for Alaska in a few days. If I remember right, I forgot to tell our employees about the trip until we were on the way. Marlene always claimed I had poor communication skills, perhaps she has a point.

25

Our trip plans were very simple. First stop, our second office in Winesburg, Ohio to check in and see how things were going there. (If I recall, that stop was when Leon, our manager, realized we were heading for Alaska. I have vowed since to be more open with him) Our second stop, Le Roy, Minnesota, to visit some friends there. Our third stop, Fairfield, Montana, to visit more friends. Then on to Seattle, Washington, up through British Columbia, Yukon, and then Alaska. (Once you hit British Columbia you are halfway there)

Once in Alaska, our plan was to cruise up to the Artic Circle, perhaps continue on to Prudhoe Bay, as well as hit some of the southern parts of Alaska. We ended up going as far south as Soldotna, AK. Our plan was to sleep in the Limo as much as possible, and make our food along side the road on our little propane cook stove. We learned many things about Alaska travel, which we will share throughout the book.

Concerned about being mauled by bears, I decided to take a pump action 12 gauge shotgun along. I was surprised how easy it actually was to take a firearm across international borders. At least Canadian borders, I doubt Mexico is nearly as accommodating. A hint: Don't take anything that looks remotely like a military gun, and no handguns. While you can legally transport hand guns through Canada, it requires a lot more paper work, and approval ahead of time. If you want to carry a handgun in Alaska, I suggest shipping it up via UPS.

We started off June 5th, 2013. Our trip was fairly uneventful for the first few hundred miles. We did have an amusing incident with a talkative toll booth operator on the Ohio turnpike. He was very interested in our trip and chatted for awhile. It turns out driving around in a camouflage limousine is a serious catalyst for conversation. If you don't like talking nonstop with complete strangers, then driving this car is not for you.

There was also some misunderstandings caused by the car's large lettering. Many folks assumed "AmericanGunDogs.com" was some sort of 2nd amendment organization. (while we are certainly for gun ownership, our website is about hunting dogs) As a result, we had people cheering and hollering many times, as if we were an NRA rally on wheels.

One complication we did have early on in the trip was caused by what I thought was brilliant innovation. Wanting to save money (after all, I consider myself frugal) I decided to simply setup my desktop computer in the limo. I did not have a good laptop, and thought this would save me money and the hassle of buying one. With 5 children in the back of the limo, this setup did not even survive the six hour drive to our Ohio office. By the time we pulled into Winesburg, my screen was cracked, and other components were showing serious signs of early wear. So I ended up buying a laptop anyway at a WalMart.

Somewhere near Elkhart, Indiana, we decided to stop for the night. We pulled into a campground just at closing time, with barely enough time to get a camp spot. We had not eaten supper yet, so I bought a pack of hot dogs at the office, while checking in. It turns out the family had other plans, and refused to eat my over priced hotdogs. So we drove around, but we could not find any restaurants open, except a McDonalds.

The next day, we headed for LeRoy, Minnesota. Our friends, Micah and Lori (and their family), had moved out there from Pennsylvania a year or two ago. We thought it would be great to connect with them again, and the free lodging was also a plus. On the way, we ignorantly followed the GPS through Chicago. Chicago is one city you want to avoid at all costs, drive 100 miles out of the way to avoid it, if needed. You'll save money, and probably time. It seemed like every mile or two we had to

AmericanGunDogs.com blog post by Matt on 6/04/2013:

A journey of 10,000 miles begins with...

A journey of 10,000 miles begins with lots of horsing around. If we follow our planned route to Prudhoe Bay, Alaska, and back it will be over 10,000 miles. But anyway, we are loaded and ready to head out tomorrow morning!

The Limo is in tip top shape, we took a few precautions, including:

- Replaced the fuel pump
- Replaced the crankshaft censor
- Installed the hitch (which we took off our ailing Ford Expedition)
- Wired in my desktop computer (my laptop is on deaths doorstep)
- Purchased a GPS that had a Canadian map
- Wired up a 2500 watt invertor
- Replaced the battery
- Flush tranny fluid
- Purchased a new 12 gauge Mossberg Slug Gun from Beavertown G & G
- Purchased a new camp stove
- Lined up dog sitters for our fine hunting dogs
- Tinted all the windows
- Spent several hours contacting various Canadian offices to secure proper forms for taking a firearm into Canada

On the road! The view of the back of the Limo from up front

stop and throw money in their stupid toll machines. Most of the toll is a dollar here and a dollar there, but it really adds up. I think we wasted over $100 on toll driving through that cesspool. Chicago drivers also drive like they have lost their minds. We did stop at a Cracker Barrel near Chicago, and the people there were actually friendly.

We arrived in LeRoy, Minnesota just in time for supper. Micah and Lori actually had a separate building with guest quarters in it, which made it seem like a bed and breakfast. Our sons, Shane and Rylan, hit it off very well. They both liked climbing trees and shooting things. (with a toy bow and arrow)

The next morning we hit the road again. Micah and Lori suggested stopping in at Walnut Grove, one of the towns where Laura Ingalls Wilder lived, in the book "Along the Banks of Plum Creek", part of the "Little House on the Prairie" series.

Micah and Lori and their family

Our family in front of the Limo in LeRoy, Minnesota

I have to admit, being a fan of the "Little House" book series, I was just as exited as the children to see Plum Creek and the site of the dug out home the Ingalls lived in. Below you can see Shane, Desiree and Kallia on the "big" rock Laura writes about. Plum Creek is right behind them.

The dugout has collapsed, however the area where it was is outlined for visitors to see. I decided that I had nothing to complain about, my house is huge compared to this!

From Walnut Grove, we headed north. We did some sight seeing in North Dakota, stopping at one place to take a walk on a short trail to an overlook. The picture below was taken there. On

our way back to the limo, we noticed a small crowd around our car, taking pictures. I must admit to feeling a bit self conscious walking up and getting back in with all those people gawking. I guess that's just part of driving fine automotive machinery around.

After driving through North Dakota, we eventually rolled into Montana. We were finally in "Big Sky" country, although North Dakota has it's share of "Big Sky" too. I was amazed how empty Montana actually is. We drove for miles and miles, often going 70 or 80 miles between towns. Of course, we hadn't seen anything yet. Our most humorous experience in Montana was in a little one horse town, I don't remember the name, but it was several hours of driving inside the state line.

We were driving through a side street, looking for a motel or hotel to stop at. Suddenly, we seen a fellow that looked like an authentic cowboy come running out of a garage, pointing at the limo and shouting. He was holding his hat on his head as he ran. Three or four more cowboys came running out of the garage, but by the time they were outside we were almost out of sight. I guess they don't get many limos through those parts.

After seeing quite a few scary looking motels, we finally slept in the limo for the night. In the picture below I am standing on the car hood, keeping a lookout while one of the children did their business in the bushes beside the road.

We arrived in Fairfield, Montana the next day. Our friends, Laban and Jolene, lived there. They used to be our neighbors in Middleburg, Pa, but wisely chose not to resist the urge of moving to more rural country. Below you can see the view from their front yard.

We stayed at Laban and Jolene's for one night. We got a tour of the neighborhood, and also got a chance at some gopher hunting. Unfortunately, Laban did not have much ammunition on hand. Not wanting to be a bother, I just used the only gun I had along, a 12 gauge shotgun. My ammunition selection was only brown bear loads, 660 grain 3 inch magnum slugs. Those little critters turned out to be pretty hard to hit, and I succeeded only in making craters in the ground. At $3 a bullet, I didn't make very many craters, either.

After leaving Laban's we headed out across the remainder of Montana, through Idaho, and into

Washington state. This was my first time in Washington, however Marlene had seen it before. One highlight here was stopping at Puget Sound. It was very windy, and it seemed like we needed to hang on to the children to keep them from blowing away, as you can see in the photo below:

The scenery here truly was beautiful! It was a bit chilly though, and with the high wind, it made us go back to the limo before long. The scale

of how big the sound is does not show up on photos. You'll have to make the trip yourself sometime....

Marlene does have one regret about our drive through Washington State. She wished she would have sampled a cow pie at Cow Creek. A "cow pie" is actually a type of dessert that looks very tasty. I'm not sure if we were feeling cheap, or what the deal was, but we passed up our chance to try one, and now we have to wait until we get through there again. (who knows how many years that could be) Next stop: Canada.

Chapter 4

Our next leg of the trip was the border crossing into Canada. I was a little nervous for several reasons. One, I had a shotgun in the trunk. Yes, it was legal, at least to the best of my knowledge. Second, I was driving a limousine painted camouflage. Third, we had 7 people in the car (our whole family) which should not be any problem, considering we all had passports. However this kind of thing makes me nervous, no matter how much time I prepared.

We crossed at the border crossing close to Seattle. As the car rolled up to the window, the guard did not seem to bat an eyelid. I gave him all the passports, told him we had a firearm in the trunk, and answered all his questions. He told us to park the car, leave the shotgun in the trunk, and bring everyone in the building.

You need a special form filled out ahead of time, in order to bring a gun into Canada. I brought this form, (which I had filled out before we left) in triplicate, into the building along with Marlene and the children. I gave this form to a stern looking woman, who typed a bunch of things into her computer. I was surprised how little time the whole process took. After about five minutes, she informed me the border guards needed to checkout the gun, and two of them  went out to the car. Unfortunately they couldn't get the car trunk open, and I had to go out and help them open it.

After they verified the serial number on the gun matched the serial number on the paperwork, I was given a 60 day permit to transport and possess firearms in Canada. This also let me purchase ammunition, if I wanted to. The permit cost $25 Canadian, I believe.

The picture below we took soon after entering Canada, in British Columbia. At this point we had driven a little over 3,000 miles. The limo was running excellent, and getting over 22 mpg on each tank of gas that I checked.

Our first night in Canada we stopped at a campground and rented an RV spot, and parked the limo there. The folks camping in the spot beside us appeared to be drinking, and made loud exclamations when we pulled in. We found this was going to be the usual response anywhere we went in Canada. (the loud exclamations, not the drinking) Overall we found the Canadians to be more friendly than Americans, despite the fact that some hinted we desecrated their flag with our camouflage pattern. (sorry I didn't think of it when I used maple leaves for stencils)

Later, when I repainted the limo a second time, I was

careful to use a more politically correct camouflage paint scheme. I also used "real" automotive paint.

Canada turned out even more beautiful than we anticipated.

A north British Columbia fuel station

After 3,000 plus miles– we still were not on the Alaskan Highway! But getting close!

One of the most miserable nights on the whole trip was spent at this campground below. I don't remember the name of the campground, but it was close to Yukon. It was at this point in the trip the mosquitos got really, really bad. Up until now I thought all the mosquito lore we had heard about was just hear say. Here we learned that it was true. All night we had mosquitos buzzing around our heads, somewhere they were finding their way in the car.

Around 5am, with blood splattered from squished mosquitos over every window in the limo, we hit the road. The mosquitos were so bad outside the car that most of the people in the campground were wearing mosquito nets. Further north the mosquitos were still bad, but not as bad as this spot, I don't know why they were so bad here, if the lake had something to do with it, or what. (the next time we drove north we took a case of mosquito coils along)

Later down the road, we were astonished at this pictur-
esque scene. The lake was smooth as glass. We stopped right in
the middle of the road to take this picture, not much traffic around
in northern British Columbia.

We were disappointed with the wildlife, at first. However
once we started seeing bears, they wouldn't stop. Below is a picture of the first black
bear we seen on the
trip. Soon, however,
they became so com-
mon we didn't even
stop anymore. Brown
bears were elusive on
this trip, we only seen
two on the entire trip.
We did not see any

moose until we crossed over into Alaska.

Part of the joys of traveling through northern Canada is that it takes awhile to get anywhere. With scenery this nice, it would be a shame if it didn't last long.

Keep in mind the signs you are looking at in Canada are in Kilometers, which are roughly half a mile. So it does seem like you are really making good time. As you can see in the sign below, we are almost 150 miles away from the actual Alaskan Highway, or "ALCAN" highway. The ALCAN highway starts in Dawson Creek, British Columbia, and runs to Delta Junction, Alaska. The entire length of the highway is 1,387 miles. Construction of the highway was started in 1942, as the United States needed a land route to Alaska in case of a Japanese invasion.

The picture on the next page was taken by standing out the sunroof of the limo. This turned out to be an excellent way to see the scenery.

DISTANCE CHART

SOUTH TO	km
40 MILE FLATS	
ISKUT	5
NEXT REST AREA (SUMMER ONLY)	17
TATOGGA LAKE	27
KINISKAN LAKE PARK	33
NEXT REST AREA (YEAR ROUND)	58
BOB QUINN LAKE	78
BELL II	126
MEZIADIN JUNCTION	174
STEWART	267
KITWANGA	329
YELLOWHEAD HIGHWAY	419

NORTH TO	km
NEXT REST AREA (SUMMER ONLY)	38
DEASE LAKE	65
NEXT REST AREA (YEAR ROUND)	185
TELEGRAPH CREEK	194
GOODHOPE LAKE	203
BOYA LAKE PARK	216
ALASKA HIGHWAY	301

Wikipedia states that the entire ALCAN highway is paved. I can vouch that this is not true, the photo below was taken on the ALCAN, and that is not pavement you see there. In fact, this truck roared past us, breaking our windshield in 2 places from flying stones. If you drive to Alaska, just plan on replacing your windshield, it's pretty much inevitable.

Yukon Ho! We finally found that mysterious place that Calvin and Hobbes were looking for. Below is a lake outside of Whitehorse, Yukon. If I ever lived in Canada, it would be in the Yukon. It rivals Alaska in huge expanse of wilderness and mountains. To be fair, so does British Columbia, but Yukon is even more remote.

Buckshot Betty's is the last stop before Alaska. It's 18 miles to the Alaska border from here. The children do seem to be getting tired of sitting at this point, but they have traveled very well. We are all very excited to see "Welcome to Alaska". If you're driving through here, be sure to stop at Buckshot Betty's, the food is good, priced right, and it's the only place around...

Alaska!

Chapter 5

It was hard to believe we were finally in Alaska! The children ran around in excitement. (I think Marlene and I might have to) After all the excitement of getting out and looking at the Alaska sign, it was time to go through customs back into the United States. In one book I read, a guy from Ohio drives a tractor to Alaska. It records the border guard's astonished expression and comments when the farm tractor rolled up the border crossing station.

Perhaps we had the same border guard, because this guard was also incredulous. He exclaimed he had "never seen anything like this come through before". He also cautioned me that people up here "take their guns seriously" and that I wouldn't want to appear to be in favor of gun control.

I don't know what made the border guard think I was advocating confiscation of Alaskan's firearms, but I quickly assured him I was all for owning guns, but in fact, our business was about dogs, not guns. I even told him I had a shotgun in the trunk. He still seemed to think I was some kind of liberal, freedom hating type from the eastern seaboard, however he let us through. The total time at the border checkpoint was probably less than 10 minutes.

Upon arriving in Alaska, the first town you come to is Tok, pronounced "Toke". After Tok, it's pretty much just open wilderness. It was getting late in the day when we arrived, but we kept driving and just slept in the limo again.

We noticed that Alaska is indeed "The land of the midnight sun". The picture we took below is of the first moose we seen. It was taken after 11 pm. We drove until 1 in the morning without turning our headlights on. It did get a little on the dark side after that, however when we drove up to Prudhoe Bay, the sun shone as brightly at midnight as did at noon.

We arrived in Wasilla, Alaska, the following day. The temperature was 105 degrees. We were shocked, I always thought of Alaska as being a little nippier than this. Our motel we stayed in had no air conditioning, and we sweated like horses. I was later told this was a 50 year heat record. I had heard that Sarah Palin lived in Wasilla, and I thought maybe we would see her, assuming that all towns in Alaska were comprised of tiny little huts in a circle. I was shocked to discover that Wasilla was actually very populated, and we never did see Sarah Palin.

Our plans were to rent a cabin for a few days once we arrived in Alaska. After calling a few cabin rental places, I realized we might have trouble. They were all full, except one place that threw fits about the amount of children we had. I tried explaining that we spent 10 days in a limousine, so we certainly could fit in a cabin for a few days, but this logic fell on deaf, tyrannical ears.

We had some friends of friends in Sterling, who gave us the number of "Cozy Cabins" a cabin rental place in Sterling.

Being completely ignorant of Alaskan geography, I typed "Sterling" into Google maps, and it showed a 20 minute drive. So we booked the cabin for 4 days, and loaded up the limo. To our shock, after programming the car GPS, it showed a 5+ hour drive! Having already make a deposit over the phone to hold the cabin, we decided to go anyway. After driving over 80 hours, what is another 5?

We spent four days in the cabin on the previous page. It was small, but we all fit. Thankfully, Ed Scott, the owner, was reasonable and did not see any problem with having five children in the cabin. As an added plus, the Kenai river was within walking distance of the cabin. Finally we could get out of the car for a few days, and experience the truly great Alaskan outdoors. And because it did not get dark, we could hike and fish round the clock if we wanted to.

And finally, I could take the 12 gauge out of the trunk and put it to good use. We took this gun with everywhere we went, and nobody even looked twice. Another great thing about Alaska! If your one of those homicidal nuts that hates guns and prefers being eaten, or watching your children get eaten, that's your choice. Don't worry, you're not alone, quite a few people with those same views have been mauled and killed by brown bears. It's not really a bad thing if you like getting used to artificial limbs or enjoy that "scar face" look.

Tips on avoiding dismemberment in the Alaskan Wilderness; Mace, Bacon bits, and other seasonings AmericanGunDogs.com blog post

I have a friend named Alvin, who several years ago was in Alaska hunting. He was charged by a Grizzly bear, and shot it with his 30.06.

A common thread running among blogs regarding hiking, camping, fishing, and other remote out door activities in Alaska is how to avoid getting mauled (and maybe even killed) by a Grizzly bear. This is a natural fear, since the largest Grizzly bears can stand 10 feet tall on their hind legs, and can be 5 feet high on all fours, and weigh 1,400 pounds. It is also the largest land based predator in North America. (depending on your variation of Grizzly bear, or Brown bear, which is tied with the Polar Bear) The bottom line is they can eat you for lunch, literally.

The disturbing advice accompanying the thread is this: Don't worry about Grizzly bears, simply learn how they think, if one approaches you, simply grunt in Grizzly bear language. If explaining (with grunts and hand motions I guess) that you don't want to hurt the grizzly bear fails to cause it to leave, pull out a can of mace and give it a squirt in the face. Don't even consider carrying a gun, because 90% of the time you won't need it. In fact, I quote:

"Contrary to the belief of some (intelligent people), firearms are not needed for protection from bears, and studies have shown that pepper spray may actually be more effective in preventing a bear attack than firearms."

And, on the same page:

"Pepper spray has been shown to be effective at deterring grizzly bears over 90% of the time."

http://www.nps.gov/dena/frequently-asked-questions-regarding-bears.htm

Quick question here- what about the other 10% of the time? Should you go out screaming and kicking? Or quietly without a fight, since kicking and screaming is so undignified? (although having your organs littered all over the ground is undignified in any culture, especially in Alaska)

Would you drive a car that the brakes worked 90% of the time? Would you fly in airplanes that landed safely 90% of the time? Would you eat somewhere that 90% of the time you didn't get food poisoning? Would you sleep comfortably in your bed knowing that 10% of the time there was a rattlesnake in it? Would you be happy knowing that 90% of the time there wasn't an ax murderer lurking in your house?

I think we can safely say that the folks recommending you don't carry a gun in the Alaskan Wilderness would be thrown out of any other field of reasoning with their homicidal logic. In fact it is obvious they would rather see you die than a bear. If you don't carry a gun, (and go into the Alaskan wilderness for an extended period of time) here are my tips:

- Carry lots of bacon bits. (at least these won't upset the bears)
- Carry a steel tag with your id etched in it, attached to each limb. (so they know which parts belong to you when they find you)
- Make sure to wear cotton clothes, or something biodegradable.
- Have a qualified attorney write your will.
- Don't carry a recorder, it will upset your next of kin if they hear you screaming as you get mauled like that insane "live with the bears" guy.
- Leave the children at home, along with any pets.
- Max out your credit cards before heading off into the wilderness.
- Spray Mace on yourself when approached by a bear, you won't taste as good. (unless it's a Mexican Bear)

If you do carry a gun, make sure it's big enough. 12 Gauge 3 inch mag slugs are known to be most effective. Worse than pepper spray is a small caliber gun that will only enrage the bear. A 9mm may only cause mild annoying injuries to a grizzly, in fact most handguns are too small. Even a .44 Magnum lacks the stopping power to drop a big bear in it's tracks. A 12 Gauge shotgun is also easier to handle than huge bore handguns. Now, if you do carry a gun, also keep in mind:

- Don't just shoot bears if you see them, that's called poaching.
- Shooting bears should be considered a last ditch resort. (Hint: you don't need a scope to hit in these situations)
- Be careful with your gun, when I recommend carrying one I'm assuming your not a mindless idiot.
- Brenneke slugs are rumored to be the best-but I have never shot a bear so I don't know for sure.
- Make sure your shotgun does not have a full choke, this would be a bad time for your gun to explode.
- You need to be familiar with your firearm, and how to use it, before flirting with death.
- Follow the laws when carrying your firearm, be familiar with regulations in the area you are going.
- If you do shoot a bear, bear in mind you will face an extensive legal process, and possible fines, even in the event of clear self defense. My friend Alvin actually had to go before a judge and plead his case, and managed to avoid a year in jail.

And, I do like bears. I'm not out to go blast them unless it's that or be eaten. Staying alive is only one small (albeit important) facet of the great outdoors.

Fishing in Alaska needs to be timed with the salmon runs, or you won't catch any fish, at least no salmon. While we were there, the King Salmon were running. (mid June) In the picture below we are hiking down to the Kenai river. The mosquitos were particularly bad in this stretch of woods.

I purchased my fishing rig at a WalMart. The stores in Alaska are amazing, rows of rifles, pistols, and more ammunition than you can imagine. Big bore guns, such as .375 H & H, .454 Casull, 500 S & W, are common place. Also, the fishing and camping sections are equally massive. Alaska is truly a sportsman's dream. Buying my fishing license proved to have some long range ramifications. I had to choose either "resident" or "nonresident". Wow, I thought, people actually live here!! Duh, I knew that before, but it only sank in there. I decided sometime-I would be buying the "resident" fishing license. And not just to save money, either...

Fortunately our host at Alaska Cozy cabins was an excellent fisherman. Friday night he had a fish fry, and everyone at the cabins was invited. He served Halibut, something I had heard of before, but never tasted. It was a life changing experience, as I have never eaten anything as good before or since that evening!

Sweet, succulent manna from the sea- Halibut. Like most foods, it's best breaded and deep fried. It's worth driving to Alaska just for a dish of fresh Halibut, it's that good! Below, our host Ed Scott, gets the deep fryer ready for another round. To make reservations at Alaska Cozy Cabins call (907) 252-0447 , we highly recommend them.

After our stay at Alaska Cozy Cabins, it was time to head home. But first we decided to swing up to the Arctic circle and get some pictures in front of the "Arctic Circle" sign. We ate supper at this Denny's in Fairbanks.

It was around Fairbanks I noticed our first hint of trouble with the limo. (except for the windshield wipers, they had already started causing problems in North Dakota) The limo would hesitate a bit before the starter turned over. Concerned that I was experiencing alternator problems, I did what any intelligent person would do. I bought a spare battery at Fred Myer, then we started the trek from Fairbanks to the Arctic circle, through 198 miles of tundra and barren wasteland on the Dalton Highway.

The above photo was taken in the middle of the night, above Fairbanks, but still about 400 miles south of Prudhoe Bay. The closer you got to the top of Alaska, the brighter the skies.

Once we arrived at the Arctic Circle sign, we agreed our trip had reached its furthest point. We were tired of driving, and it was time to go home. Since the closest motel was back in Fairbanks, 200 miles away, we decided to just sleep in the Limo, at the pull off for the Arctic Circle sign.

As we awoke the next morning, we faced a dilemma. A nagging thought was in the back of our brains. We had not gone to the top, to Prudhoe Bay. We both agreed if we turned around now, this would eventually drive us crazy, forcing us to retrace our entire route and go to the top of Alaska, to Prudhoe Bay. A half hearted tour of Alaska would not be sufficient. So with renewed zeal, we pulled the gear shift into "drive" and once again pointed the limo "North".

The trees get progressively shorter the further north you go. The terrain got even more rugged, and the road was completely gravel, except for short paved stretches here and there. It was a blast to drive on, it was like being able to drive hundreds of miles on field lanes. (with no farmer wives around to shout at you)

The Dalton highway follows the Trans-Alaska pipeline, which brings oil down from Prudhoe Bay to Valdez. Coldfoot is a town (with a population of 10) located halfway between Fairbanks and Prudhoe Bay. During the drive from Coldfoot to Prudhoe Bay, we had to wait several hours on road construction. In the hour we waited at the one spot, only one other car came up behind us.

Below is a picture of the town of Cold Foot, Alaska:

If you have never been to Prudhoe Bay, you really are not missing much. Imagine a vast expense of tundra with equipment parked everywhere.

It's also not exactly a tourist town. We arrived just as the only store in

Kallia after waiting one hour on road construction

town was closing, either 8 or 9 pm.   That was ok, we weren't really souvenir shopping. We noticed the fuel in Prudhoe Bay was significantly more expensive than anywhere else in Alaska, and I'm afraid the souvenirs would have been as well.   Considering the closest gas station was in Coldfoot, 240 miles away, I guess the competition is sparse. This is really good country to carry gas cans, we used ours a number of times. If you run out of gas, you're in a bad, bad spot.

A DOT official flagged us down soon after we entered Prudhoe Bay, and wanted to know what we were doing there. He confirmed this was a historical moment, saying there was no record of a stretch limousine ever driving through Prudhoe Bay before. About 10 more people told us this exact same thing before we left town. Sadly, it seemed there was no trophy, formal award, or large cash prize for this accomplishment.

We couldn't find a motel in Prudhoe Bay, and it appeared there was not much to see, so we headed south again. Around 4 am we stopped at a small creek named "Gold Creek" and decided to try our hand at gold panning. This turned out to be a chilly failure, but Shane and I had fun trying, while the others slept in the car. I was hoping to see a brown bear while we were down wading in the creek, but none showed up. We were also far enough north to see polar bears, but we didn't see any of them either.

It occurred to me it might be a rather stressful situation if the car broke down, but I didn't think much about it. No need to cry over milk that had not spilt. We did have an incident with a flat tire, but a truck driver helped us plug it and fill the tire up again with air.

I have forgotten the truck drivers name, but I did not forget his dog. He had an "English War Dog" along in his truck

which, as you can see in the picture below, is a huge dog. He claimed to have four more at home. I guess he probably doesn't have problems with burglars. I did have a spare tire along, of course, but the truck driver explained that by patching the original, it saved the spare for a later time. Good Alaskan thinking. Note the guy in the picture below looking at his exhaust pipe. The whole time we stopped he was obsessing over his muffler. (like 15+ minutes) Strange.

We ran into a little rain, not much, but enough to make the road sloppy. I'm glad it didn't rain torrents, it may have left us wishing for four wheel drive. Our truck driver friend said they run trucks all year round, up and down the Dalton highway. I bet some of those winter months get pretty interesting.

Our drive back through the Dalton highway was uneventful, and we made our way to the North Pole. North Pole, Alaska, that is. This sign was hilarious, I felt like vandalizing something just to see if some elves would show up.

Registration forms are Located on Park & Sell Sign

Joesi's Park & Sell

When selecting a location to sell your auto etc. please be aware that occasionally you may have as many as 5 showing' before a sale. So always choose the Location nearest your home.

This lot is Patrolled by North Pole Police D...

Not surprisingly, the town of "North Pole" has a decidedly Christmas theme. We stayed one night at the "Hotel North Pole", and it was one of the nicest hotels we slept in on the entire trip. They even gave out free cookies. There were some rather strange looking buildings around here as well.

We decided to catch the "Top of the World Highway" on the way back home. This led us through the little town of "Chicken", which is in the heart of gold panning country. The true story of "Tisha" took place in Chicken, you can go see the school house that she taught in. Unfortunately, I read the book after I was in Chicken, so I missed that highlight. One part about Chicken I didn't like, it seemed like their town slogan was written by a pervert.

Here you can see a "Homeland Security" police rig parked beside the limo in Chicken. I suspect they parked there because they were jealous. In the picture below you can see the "Top of the World Highway" stretching out in front of the limo. This is truly a road less traveled.

Chapter 5

The day the Limo broke down

The border crossing was uneventful, in fact it was the quickest crossing yet. The border guard glanced at my firearms form, looked at the passports, and waved us through. He didn't even look inside the car. Dirt road border crossings are the way to go.

A few miles down the road, in Canada, the limo shut off, and would not start again. I tested the fuel pressure, and sure enough, it was something with the fuel system. A couple stopped to see if we needed help, and we reluctantly told them to send a tow truck from Dawson City, when they got there. We had no

phone service out here, so calling anyone was out of the question. The nearest town was Dawson City, which was around 20 miles away. After we were sitting about half an hour, Marlene decided to try and start the car again. It worked! We quick jumped in, and were on our way again, before it had a chance to break down again.

As we pulled into Dawson City to the ferry, we met a police officer and a tow truck coming the other way. We thanked them and told them we no longer needed a lift. They were very cordial, and

did not charge us anything for their time. The ferry operators told us that this was the first stretch limo ever to ride across the river. Sadly, no cash prize here either...

We considered staying the night in Dawson City, but foolishly decided to just drive on, assuming that if the car started working again, any future breakdowns would just require patience. Cruising through Dawson "City", which has a population of 1,319. We noticed all the garages were closed. It was around 9 pm, so I guess that was to be expected.

There was a nice Chinese restaurant in town, where we ate supper at before continuing on. I should have looked at the map before we left, the next town was Whitehorse, about 330 miles away. (yes, looking back I sound like a real idiot) Hey, we had extra gas cans, so why worry?

The limo purred gracefully on out of Dawson City, and ran nicely until we were in the middle of the wilderness. We had went perhaps 100 miles, when suddenly the car shut off again. It was around 10 or 11 pm, and the sun was going down, although our location was still far enough north that it didn't get real dark.

After about 30 minutes, I tried starting the car again. No success, it wouldn't start. Putting my ear against the gas tank, I couldn't hear the fuel pump run. We had just put a new fuel pump in before leaving PA, so was fairly certain the fuel pump was not the issue. We had, however, had trouble with the wiring harness on the fuel pump. My buddy, Arlan, from Clark Hill Service Center, had securely attached the wiring harness with some high dollar gasket compound of some sort. I stupidly wretched apart the harness and tested the wires for juice with a test light. No electric at the fuel pump. And now I had just wrecked Arlan's special concoction to keep the harness together.

Looking over all the fuses and relays for the fuel pump, I didn't see anything amiss. The emergency fuel shutoff switch was also good. But the power line to the fuel pump was completely dead. As I stood there, staring into the trunk of the limo, with tools scattered around me, I felt like a real failure as a father. Would we all die here, stranded along the road? Would vultures strip our carcasses clean? No, that sounds like questions one of those stupid reality TV shows would ask. I didn't think we were going to die, but I did feel like we were going to be seriously inconvenienced!

We were stuck beside the road for about 2 hours while I scratched my head and tried to figure out what to do. Three or four cars came along during that time, some expressing surprise at seeing a limousine broke down in the wilderness. I assured them at this point we were still fine, and they should not worry about us. I figured if they told the police in Dawson Creek, they would think "those idiots again!". While sitting by the road, I took this picture. It was completely silent, not a vehicle around. It's hard to enjoy the silence when you actually wish there were some more vehicles around.

After giving the situation some thought, I remembered I had a spare battery in the trunk. So I took the power wire going to the fuel pump, cut it off, and attached it to the battery. Immediately I heard the glorious hum of the fuel pump. I casually slid in the car, turned the ignition, and the car started right up! The rest of the family tried to mask their astonishment that I had actually fixed something. I do remember hearing some very congratulatory remarks.

Our exuberance was short lived, as a few miles down the road, the limo shut off again. The battery still had juice, but I had opened up Pandora's box of electrical issues by taking apart Arlan's rigged up wiring harness connection to the fuel pump. Even though I put it back together, it would not stay together for more than a few minutes, as I did not have any of the gasket compound Arlan had used to keep it together.

In what was to become a very familiar ritual, I crawled underneath the car and wiggled the wiring harness. (which you can see on the previous page) The fuel pump fired right up again. Driving through the wilderness with a car that would randomly shut off, requiring a quick trip under the gas tank to wiggle the connection, was not a big deal. However, we soon learned that it was a big deal in town.

We also faced the issue of the battery in the trunk eventually going dead. After arriving in Whitehorse, I spent some time rewiring the car. The air suspension was optional, compared to the fuel pump, so I disconnected the hot wire for that and connected it to the fuel pump instead. That worked for the rest of the trip. However the wiring harness disconnected at least a dozen times, until I got thoroughly tired of the random stopping. Checking at a NAPA somewhere in Alberta, I was informed that they did not have any wiring harnesses for the Lincoln. However they did have various sized springs and wire ties, which I fastened around the wiring harness plug. This worked the rest of the trip back to Pa. In fact, I figured why fix what works. The springs and wire tie rig has also went to Georgia, Texas, and back to Alaska again. (with only a few stops in between to crawl underneath and wiggle it)

From Alberta to Pennsylvania was uneventful. We did get to see the "Sign Post Forest" started in 1943 Private Carl K, Lindley, who was homesick for Illinois, of all places. He added a sign pointing to his hometown. The rest is history, with thieves and vandals stealing signs from their hometowns to put there ever since. (although Private Lindley was not from Chicago)

We also witnessed huge bison lumbering along the road. You don't want to hit one of these things with your car!

I remember a phone conversion Marlene had with her mom on the way back, near Chicago. Marlene remarked "we are almost home!" Most folks from Pa wouldn't consider that "almost home", unless they had just driven for a few days.

After we crossed through the battle zone of homicidal drivers in Chicago, the rest of the trip back did not seem to take long. After experiencing the wonder of the North, the lower 48 seems fairly bland (with the exception of some western states), in fact I didn't take any pictures after we crossed back into the US.

Arriving home, we were met with this sign across our driveway. We also found our refrigerator stocked. It was a long drive, but it was good to be home. After all, this was a once of a lifetime trip? This GPS I bought right before we left. I'm not sure where we hit 87-but the mileage shown is how far we drove on this particular trip.

Alaska Road Trip Survival Guide

So you want to drive to Alaska from the lower 48? Great! Here are some pages of tips and tricks to help make the trip easier (and maybe cheaper) for you, as well as lower potential mortality rates. A check list of things you consider, with more detailed explanations on the following pages:

1. Roadside assistance and towing insurance.
2. Two spare tires.
3. Make sure your spare tire(s) are not flat.
4. Take extra fluids, oil, brake fluid, etc.
5. Make sure to take extra food and water along.
6. Buy a GPS with Canada and Alaska maps. Make sure it is updated.
7. Make sure to have plenty of camera batteries and memory cards.
8. Get a Canadian plan for your cell phone.
9. Consider a CB radio.
10. Take a tire plug kit along.
11. If pulling a trailer, change all the tires to radial tires before leaving. Make sure your trailer has 14 inch tires or bigger.
12. Plan your route ahead of time.
13. If traveling in the winter, spring, or fall take snow chains or snow tires.
14. Consider an extra car battery or battery booster.
15. Call your credit card company before leaving-if not, your card will be shut down.
16. If taking a firearm, make sure it is legal in Canada. Also know you may not be able to buy one in Alaska. (depending on your home state)
17. Take your vehicle title along.
18. Don't forget a passport, extra gasoline and a tool kit.

This guide should not be considered legal advice, consult your attorney before following said suggestions. (especially the parts about eating wildlife)

1. Roadside Assistance and Towing Service

It is a good idea to sign up for a service like AAA before you leave. At a minimum, make sure that you have a road side assistance plan on your vehicle with your insurance company. I use State Farm, and they have a very reasonable plan. Make sure your plan covers towing. Ask your provider specifically if it covers breakdowns in Canada, some may not.

I have been accused at times of being paranoid-a charge that may or may not be true. However, I'm pretty sure I'm right on the roadside assistance part. For example, say you break down in Yukon. How many towing companies are competing for your business there? I'm guessing not very many. Most of these roadside assistance plans are very reasonable, in the range of $40-$100 a year. Some places you are billed $4 a mile, both ways, for the tow truck. It's possible to break down hundreds of miles from a tow truck. You do the math. (Also sign up for windshield replacement insurance)

2. Two Spare Tires

Take two spare tires, because 2-1 equals 1 left.

3. Make sure your spare tire(s) are not flat.

One time I pulled out a spare tire, only to discover it was as flat as the tire I was trying to replace.

4. Take extra fluids, oil, brake fluid, etc.

Your vehicle may not be leaking fluids, right now. But it may decide to in the middle of nowhere. If you have a seal give out, or a brake line burst, that extra fluid may make a huge difference.

5. Make sure to take extra food and water along.

Alaska state law allows you eat wildlife in a crisis. If you don't take extra food along, make sure you have a gutting knife and at least a bow and arrow. Canada is not as forgiving if you eat their wildlife, it's better to try and forage for edible plants. Brown bears are not good to eat, but moose, caribou and reindeer are excellent. Animal skins also make great souvenirs or gifts. Note that weasels taste terrible and your hands will stink for days if you try to skin one.

6. Buy a GPS with Canada and Alaska maps. Make sure it is updated.

I recommend a GPS. And not a phone either. Get one that will operate without a cell phone signal, because you won't have service most of the time. Make sure your GPS has maps of Canada and Alaska, many of the cheaper models do not.

7. Make sure to have plenty of camera batteries and memory cards.

Your taking a road trip that will have a thousand photo quality moments, looking at scenery people often only dream about.

Make sure your camera works!

8. Get a Canada plan for your cell phone.

Very, very important. You can't imagine the kind of bills you can rack up if you don't have an international plan. Default out of country data rates are like $25 a MB. Your 4G smart phone will burn up 10 MB in a few seconds. Voice calls are around $1 a minute, without a plan. I ran up $100 on my phone bill with ATT in less than 30 seconds in Grand Praire, Alberta, because I did not get a Canadian phone plan added to my service.

9. Consider a CB radio.

A handheld CB radio can be useful for summoning help in the event your cell phone does not have service.

10. Take a tire plug kit along.

Tire plug kits cost under $20. I highly recommend you purchase one and take it along, as well as a DC air compressor.

11. If pulling a trailer, change all the tires to radial tires before leaving. Make sure your trailer has 14+ inch tires.

Little tires on pop up trailers, for example, will leave a wake of shredded rubber across Canada. Don't even consider pulling anything with little tires on the rough north roads. Change all tires to radials, or you will be changing them frequently along the way, when it is not convenient! (it is usually raining when a tire blows out)

12. Plan your route ahead of time.

This is a bit of common sense. Use Google maps, an atlas, etc to figure out where you want to go before you leave. I recommend the route from Seattle, Washington, up through British Columbia. The good news is you can't go wrong, it's all beautiful.

13. If traveling in the winter, spring or fall take snow chains or snow tires.

Some north roads legally require snow chains or snow tires from October to May. It is also a good idea.

14. Consider an extra car battery or battery booster.

If your battery goes dead, your car won't start. Period. I recommend replacing your battery if it is more than 2 years old, or taking a spare along. Even if your alternator gives out, a spare battery will limp you along quite a ways.

15. Call your credit card company before leaving-if not, your card will be shut down.

Notify your credit card company that you will be traveling, or your card WILL be shut off. It is a good idea to have a couple of hundred dollars cash on hand as well. Even in Canada US dollars are often accepted.

16. If taking a firearm, make sure it is legal in Canada. Also know you may not be able to buy one in Alaska. (depending on your home state)

You can survive just fine without a gun on the drive through Canada. I, however, refuse to walk around in the forests of Canada or Alaska without a large caliber firearm. (maybe this goes back to the paranoid thing) An easy way to get your long gun to Alaska, is to send it via the postal service to AK. Handguns must be shipped via UPS or FedEx. See their websites for details.

It is easy to transport long guns through Canada, if they meet certain requirements. To be safe, I recommend they be manually operated, only hold 3 or 4 rounds, and look as tame as a kitten. No bayonet lugs, flash suppressors, or scary looking things bolted on. And no mace or bear spray allowed in Canada.

It is a bit odd Canada will trust you with a 12 gauge shotgun, but not a can of pepper spray. Thankfully it's not the other way around. Also, don't plan on buying a gun in Alaska. For example, I met some folks from New York. They planned to simply purchase a shotgun at WalMart, and take it along fishing, and then sell it again before leaving Alaska. Not so.

New York will not let it's citizens purchase firearms in other states. Not content with saddling NY residents with it's oppressive firearm laws while only in NY, the long fingers of tyranny reach the whole way to Alaska. Of course, the solution is easy. Just go down to the local Alaska DMV, hand in your NY drivers license, and get an Alaska one, with an Alaska address. And then stay. Pennsylvania residents can purchase firearms in Alaska, as of June 2014. Other states vary.

This gun will get you a grunt and nod of approval from border officials. (with proper paperwork of course)

This gun may result in an extended Canadian prison stay:

17. Take your vehicle title along.

Seriously, take your vehicle title along. There are a number of reasons for this. You may arrive in Alaska, sick of driving, and decide to sell it and fly home. Or you may decide to become a resident of Alaska, and you will need the title to get an Alaska vehicle registration. Or your car may break down and require expensive repairs, prompting you to trade it in on another one.

My one friend from Alaska drove his truck down to the lower 48. After several breakdowns, he dumped it off at a dealer and bought a new truck. I thought this was a hair extravagant, until my vehicle broke down.

18. Don't forget a passport, extra gasoline and a toolkit

Contrary to popular belief you do not need a passport to enter Canada. Usually. However it makes it easier if you do, and having a passport practically insures entry. It would really be an inconvenience if you drove the whole way to the US/Canada border crossing in Seattle, Washington, or North Dakota, and couldn't get entry into Canada. Talk about a deal breaker! It is also a good idea to have copies of your children's birth certificates. If traveling without the other parent, always have a notarized paper stating permission to take the children out of the country.

Take extra gasoline cans along. Sure, there are supposed to be gas stations open at frequent intervals all along the ALCAN highway. What are you going to do if you come to a gas station that is closed, and you are out of gas? Quote information you read on the Internet to the gas pumps? No, that doesn't work. Take at least two 5 gallon gas cans along. If you don't need the gas, great, you can always run it in the lawn mower.

Another hint: You can still buy old style gas cans in Canada, the ones without the demented "spill proof" spout. (It may be illegal to import these into the US) Ironically, the spill proof spouts often do not work right, (unless you buy the more expensive models) causing folks to take them off and try to pour gas without any spout. The result is large amounts of gasoline being dumped all over the ground, killing spotted owls and endangered rodents everywhere.

Make sure to have a basic took kit along with sockets, screw drivers, etc. Even if you are not a mechanic, someone may come along who is, and be able to use your tools to help you out.

What are you waiting for? Come experience Alaska!